The Noisy Neighbour

Luke 11: God is Good

CATHERINE MACKENZIE
Illustrated by Chiara Bertelli

CF4•K

Learn it: Every good gift is from God
Do it: Keep praying
Find it: Who should we pray for? Matthew 5:44

Imagine that you are curled up in bed. You are almost asleep. Your teeth are brushed and you've said your prayers. Your bedroom is nice and quiet. It's time to go to sleep.

Would your mother wake you up and tell you to hoover the floor? Would your dad tell you to weed the garden? What would you say to your sister if she asked you to paint her bedroom? I think you would say, 'Go to sleep everyone!' But what if someone really needed your help? What would you do?

Jesus told a story about a sleepy man who was woken up in the middle of the night. He was sound asleep. His wife was sound asleep. All his kids were sound asleep. It was very late. All of a sudden there was a loud knocking at the door. His neighbour started to shout noisily, 'Let me in. Let me in. I need some loaves of bread. A friend of mine has arrived after a long journey and I don't have anything for him to eat.'

At first the sleepy man replied, 'Go away. Don't bother me. I've locked the door and I don't want to wake the children. I can't get up and give you anything!' But the noisy neighbour kept on knocking and kept on asking until the sleepy man got out of bed, went down to the kitchen and finally opened the door. 'Take as much bread as you need,' he yawned and the noisy neighbour went away happy.

What does Jesus want us to learn from this story? Well, Jesus wants you to pray to God.

WHAT IS PRAYER? Prayer is when we tell God what we want or need. Prayer is also when we say sorry to God for disobeying him and when we say thank you to God for all the good things he has done.

In the story the noisy neighbour kept knocking and kept asking. Jesus wants us to keep praying. When we're in trouble we must ask God for help. We're not to give up. If it's something we really want we're to ask God for it.

If it's not good for us and it's not part of God's plan for us God will say, 'No'. If it's not the right time, God will say, 'Wait'. However, if what we pray for is part of God's plan he will say, 'Yes'. God is in charge.

Jesus said to his friends, the disciples, 'Suppose your little boy asks you for a fish – would you give him a snake instead? Or if he asks you for an egg would you give him a scorpion?

Even though you are evil you know how to give good gifts to your children. How much more will your Heavenly Father give the Holy Spirit to those who ask him?'

Jesus wants you to know that God is the best at giving good gifts. You can be confident that his choice is right even when he says, 'No'. God's best gift is God the Holy Spirit.

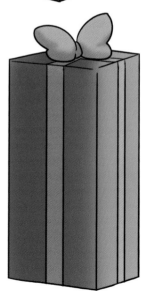

WHO IS THE HOLY SPIRIT? God is one God in three persons. God the Father, God the Son (Jesus) and God the Holy Spirit. When God gives people his Holy Spirit they want to please God instead of disobeying him. With the Holy Spirit in their lives they will go to heaven when their bodies die.

God is so precious we need to seek him and find him. When you play hide and seek you find your friends. When you seek God, you find out about the one who knows you and loves you best. God wants you to find him. You can find out about him in the Bible. Don't give up.

The noisy neighbour didn't give up. He knocked on the door and kept on knocking. He called out for bread and didn't stop until eventually his friend got out of bed.

When you pray keep praying. God is kind and loving. He is most kind and loving. He hears your prayers and will answer them.

God is kinder than the kindest friend. He is more loving than the loveliest father. You can speak to God about anything. You can pray to God at any time and in any place. The Bible tells us that we should always pray. God is always listening.

And when you pray to God have a proper conversation with him – because he is a friend. When you speak to friends you don't just ask them for things: 'Can I have your book?' 'I need to borrow your bike.' 'Please give me some of your chocolate.'

You also say things like, 'Thank you,' and 'I'm sorry.'
You tell them how much you love them.
You should say these things to God too.

You should say, 'Thank you God for loving me.'

'I'm sorry for disobeying you and not loving you like I should.'

'You are wonderful and caring and so faithful. I can be confident in you and trust you completely.'

Christian Focus Publications

Christian Focus Publications publishes books for adults and children under its four main imprints: Christian Focus, CF4K, Mentor and Christian Heritage. Our books reflect our conviction that God's Word is reliable and Jesus is the way to know him, and live for ever with him. Our children's list includes a Sunday School curriculum that covers pre-school to early teens, and puzzle and activity books. We also publish personal and family devotional titles, biographies and inspirational stories that children will love. If you are looking for quality Bible teaching for children then we have an excellent range of Bible stories and age-specific theological books. From pre-school board books to teenage apologetics, we have it covered!

AUTHOR'S DEDICATON: To my friends and family at Kingsview Christian Centre, A.P.C.

10 9 8 7 6 5 4 3 2 1
Copyright © 2017 Catherine Mackenzie
ISBN: 978-1-5271-0097-8
Published in 2017 by Christian Focus Publications Ltd.
Geanies House, Fearn, Tain, Ross-shire, IV20 1TW, Great Britain
Illustrations by Chiara Bertelli
Cover Design: Sarah Korvemaker
Printed in Malta